Bites and Stings

Dr. Alvin Silverstein,

Virginia Silverstein, and

Laura Silverstein Nunn

My Health

Franklin Watts

A Division of Scholastic Inc.

New York • Toronto • London • Auckland • Sydney

Mexico City • New Delhi • Hong Kong

Danbury, Connecticut

Photographs ©: Peter Arnold Inc.: 18 (Bios), 8 (David Scharf); Photo Researchers, NY: 13 (Biophoto Associates), 29 (Juergen Berger, Max-Planck Institute/SPL), 10 (Dr. Jeremy Burgess/SPL) 34 left (CNRI/SPL), 31 (Andy Crump, TDR, Who/SPL), 20 (Stephen Dalton), 23 (John Kaprielian), 39 (Dr. P. Marazzi/SPL), 19 (Tom McHugh), 17 right (Carolyn A. McKeone), 25 (Gregory Ochocki), 9 (Dr. H. C. Robinson/SPL), 34 right (EM Unit, CVL Weybridge/SPL); PhotoEdit: 16 (M. Ferguson), 37 (Robert Ginn), 17 left (Michael Newman); Photri: 26 (Biedel), 12 bottom (Rob & Ann Simpson); Stone: 15 (James Balog), 22 (Tom Bean), 7 (Robert Brons/BPS); Visuals Unlimited: 4 (D. Cavagnaro), 6 (Jeff Greenberg), 27, 35 (Ken Greer), 36 (Larry Jensen), 12 top (Steve Maslowski), 14 (Joe McDonald), 21 (R. A. Simpson), 24 (Marty Snyderman).

Cartoons by Rick Stromoski

Library of Congress Cataloging-in-Publication Data

Silverstein, Alvin.
    Bites and stings / by Alvin Silverstein, Virginia Silverstein, and Laura Silverstein Nunn.
        48 p.; col. ill.; 25 cm.—(My health)
    Includes bibliographical references (p. 45) and index.
    ISBN 0-531-11861-4 (lib. bdg.)   0-531-16559-0 (pbk.)
        1. Bites and stings—Juvenile literature. [1. Bites and stings. 2. Diseases.]
I. Silverstein, Virginia B. II. Nunn, Laura Silverstein. III. Title. IV. Series.

RD96.2.S556 2001
617.1—dc21   00-049989

Contents

What Bit You?

You'd know that annoying whining sound anywhere. It means there's a pesky mosquito flying around your head. You try to smack the insect, but it's too late. It has already bitten you.

You're picking flowers in the garden and notice a bee flying close to you. You try to wave it away, but the insect stings you anyway. Ouch! That bee sting really hurts.

Insects are not the only creatures that can hurt you. If you play a little too rough with your dog, it might nip you with its sharp teeth. If you are swimming in the ocean and bump into a jellyfish, you might get stung. Animals bite and sting for two reasons—to protect themselves from danger or to get food.

Did You Know...

When an animal bites you, it sinks its mouthparts into your skin. When an animal stings you, a pointed stinger on its tail shoots poison into your body. Mosquitoes, fleas, ticks, cats, dogs, and mice can bite you. Bees, wasps, jellyfish, scorpions, and stingrays can sting you.

◀ Who could resist picking such beautiful flowers? But beware, bees love them too!

A mosquito bite or a bee sting can usually be treated at home. A dog bite or a scorpion sting can be more serious. If these animals attack you, you should see a doctor right away. In some cases, you may need to go to the hospital. Sometimes it's hard to know how serious a bite or sting is. That's why you should always tell an adult about your injury.

Being attacked by a dog is not only scary, it can be dangerous. This boy needed to get stitches after he was bitten by a dog.

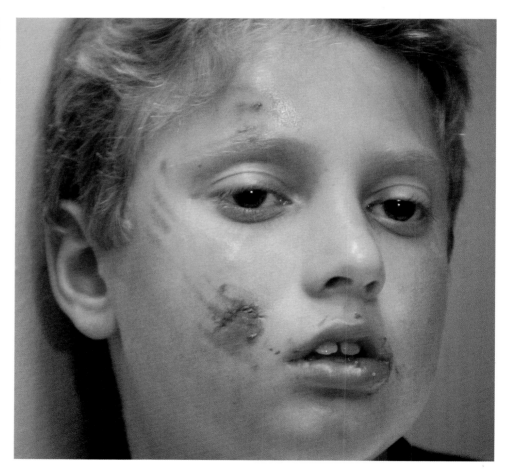

What's Bugging You?

Insects, ticks, spiders, and scorpions can be really annoying. Mosquitoes, fleas, and ticks may try to drink your blood. Bees, wasps, and scorpions can give you a painful sting. Bites from spiders and ants can hurt a lot too.

When a mosquito lands on you, it cuts into your skin with its needlelike **proboscis** (pro-BAHS-sis). As soon as it injects **saliva** into you, the bite starts to sting and itch. Mosquito saliva contains chemicals that keep blood from clotting so that it flows freely into the insect's body.

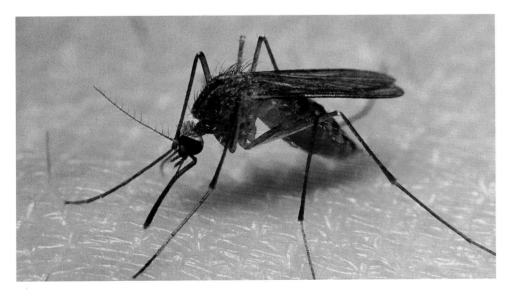

Have you ever seen a mosquito this close up? In a matter of seconds, it can pierce your skin, suck your blood, and then be on its way.

Fleas are not picky eaters. They like to feed on the blood of dogs and cats, but they are just as happy to feast on you. You may feel one of these tiny, blood-sucking insects on your skin, but they are hard to spot. And they are even harder to catch.

Fleas move fast, and they are champion jumpers. A flea can jump 8 inches (20 centimeters) high and leap as far as 13 inches (33 cm). That may not sound like a lot, but think of it this way: If a flea were the

This tiny flea is magnified 1,610 times.

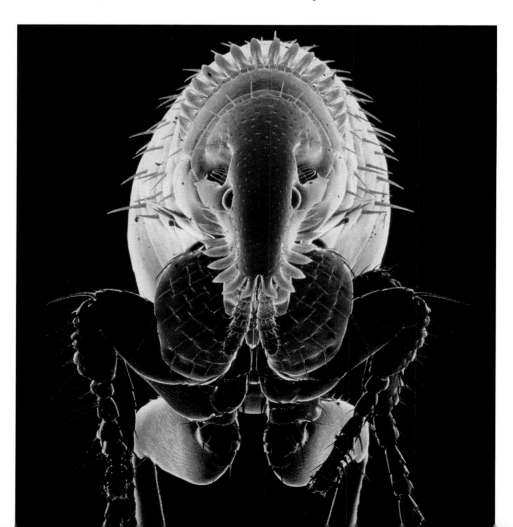

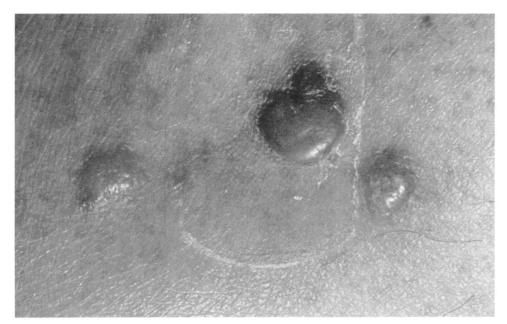

Flea bites can feel really itchy and annoying, but scratching can make them even worse.

size of a person, it would have no trouble leaping over two football fields.

A flea uses its sharp beak to pierce through skin. Then it injects saliva into the **wound** and drinks up a blood meal. Like other insect bites, flea bites are itchy and irritating.

Wasps and bees are usually attracted to sweet-smelling things and colorful patterns. That's why you often see them flying around flowers, picnic lunches, and garbage dumps. These insects do not normally attack people. But if you swat at one or disturb its nest, it may sting you.

Hornets and yellow jackets are members of the wasp family. If one of these insects stings you, it probably will not leave its stinger behind. Neither will a bumblebee. But if a honeybee stings you, it will leave its stinger—along with a tiny sac of **venom**—in your skin. Even after the bee has flown away, the stinger will continue to pump out venom. The longer the stinger stays in your skin, the more the wound will hurt. So it's important to get the stinger out as soon as possible.

If you bother a honeybee, it may sting you. When the bee flies away, it may leave its stinger in you.

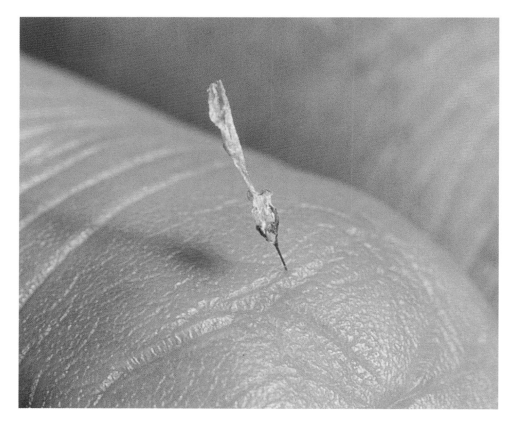

Insect Allergies

Most people are **allergic** to the chemicals in a mosquito's saliva. When they get a bite, their skin turns red, gets swollen, and feels itchy. Allergies can make other insect bites itchy too. Some people are so allergic to the venom of bees and wasps that their whole body reacts. They may faint, have trouble breathing, or even die if they are not treated right away.

All spiders use venom to kill their **prey**. But the venom of most spiders is not strong enough to hurt people. Only two kinds of dangerous spiders live in North America—the black widow spider and the brown recluse spider.

The black widow spider is most common in the southern United States. Its poisonous bite is very painful, and it can be deadly. It is easy to identify a black widow spider. Just look for a red mark shaped like an hourglass on the underside of its **abdomen**.

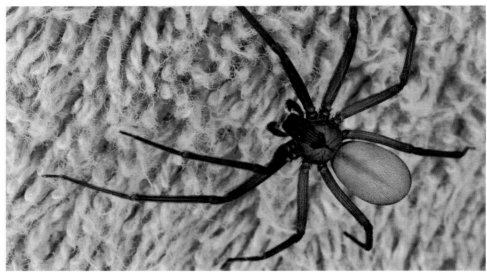

Take a look at the two most danger-ous spiders in North America: the black widow spider (top) and the brown recluse spider (bottom).

The brown recluse spider lives in the southern and central United States. It is brown and has a black mark shaped like a violin on its back. These spiders usually spin webs in dark places, such as basements or woodpiles. You might not even notice them—until you feel their painful bite. If a brown recluse spider bites you, you should go to the hospital right away.

Ticks look like tiny spiders, and the two animals are closely related. Like mosquitoes, ticks need blood to survive. Most ticks live in fields with tall grass or in wooded areas. When a person or another mammal passes by, the tick drops or crawls onto it. The tick grabs on tight with its mouthparts and starts sucking blood. A tick's saliva contains a pain-killing chemical, so you may not even know it's there. The tick may continue to feed for several hours. When it is full, the

This tick, which is attached to human skin, is full of blood.

tick drops off. Most ticks are harmless, but a few carry diseases that can make you very sick.

A scorpion uses the tip of its tail to sting enemies and capture prey. Scorpion stings often cause a lot of pain and swelling, but they are not usually dangerous. More than thirty species of scorpions live in the United States, but only one of them has venom that can kill a person.

A scorpion's stinger is on the tip of its curved tail.

Pets Can Bite

Would you believe that more people are bitten by pets than by wild animals? Dogs are known for their loyalty and devotion toward their owners, but sometimes they can get out of control. They may become **aggressive** and bite anyone nearby. A dog may even bite its owner if it is startled. Each year, dogs bite more than a million people in the United States.

You don't want to get close to an angry rottweiler. Its sharp teeth could really hurt you.

Any dog—even one that is normally calm and friendly—may bite a person if it is annoyed or startled. A dog's long, sharp teeth are made for tearing and biting meat, so a dog bite can be very serious—sometimes even deadly. Pit bulls and rottweilers are known for their aggressive behavior, but they are not as dangerous as many people think. Some kinds of dog are more likely to bite than others, but the way a dog is trained plays an important part in how it behaves toward people.

Cats may look cute and cuddly, but they can hurt you too. A playful kitten might nip you with its sharp teeth or scratch you with its razor-sharp claws. An adult cat may bite you if it feels frightened or annoyed.

Even a playful kitten can scratch or nip you.

Smaller pets might also try to bite you. Hamsters are solitary animals and normally live alone. If you annoy a hamster or wake it up from a nap, it may bite you. Gerbils are more sociable than hamsters, but they can bite too.

Tame mice and rats are very different from their wild relatives. They have been specially **bred** for gentle and friendly behavior. Most pet rats like attention, and they love to play. When mice and rats are cared for properly, they do not usually bite unless they become scared or annoyed.

You have to be gentle with pet hamsters (below), gerbils, mice, and rats (right). These little critters will bite if they get scared.

Exotic or unusual pets, such as chinchillas, fennec foxes, hedgehogs, sugar gliders, and ferrets, are getting more and more popular. Most of these animals have not been specially bred for tame behavior. They still have their wild instincts. They may be calm and friendly pets if they are handled often—and gently—when they are very young. But when exotic animals aren't raised carefully, they may be easily frightened and quick to bite.

A hedgehog won't bite—even when it's scared or annoyed. That's because it has a different kind of defense. Its body is covered with prickly spines. When a hedgehog gets nervous, it curls up in a ball with its spines sticking out. Getting stuck by one of those spines is painful. It is almost like getting stung—except that the spines do not contain poison.

Hedgehogs can be a lot of fun to play with, but you have to watch out for their prickly spines.

Dangers in the Wild

Wild animals are fun to watch, but don't get too close. Animals have to be tough to survive in the wild. They tend to bite when they are scared or nervous.

Imagine how you would feel if a giant animal followed you and cornered you so that you couldn't escape. That's how a field mouse or a chipmunk feels when a person gets too close. You might want to reach down and touch these cute animals, but that would scare them. They might bite you to protect themselves.

If you see a wild mouse in your house, don't try to catch it.

City Wildlife

If you live in a large city, you've probably seen rats. Experts say that the rat population in New York City has been as high as 30 million! Wild rats can give painful bites, which may become **infected**. They can also get into people's food and spread diseases.

A sight like this is pretty common in large cities.

Many people are afraid of bats. They think of them as vampires that come out at night and swoop down to bite the necks of their victims and suck their blood. Vampire bats do exist, but they usually feed on cows' blood. They do not normally attack humans. Most other bats eat insects or fruit.

If you find an injured bat, don't touch it. It will probably be frightened and bite you. A bat bite can be dangerous because it can spread the germs of a serious disease called **rabies**.

Raccoons look like masked bandits—and they act like them too. They are smart, curious animals. They can learn to open latches and gates. They can also take the lids off garbage cans. Raccoons are normally

active at night. If you see a raccoon wandering around during the day, it could be sick. It might bite or scratch you without warning. Like bats, raccoons may have rabies. If a raccoon bites you, you need to see a doctor immediately.

Have you ever watched a snake slithering through the grass? It may look really neat twisting and turning sideways along the ground, but don't pick it up. The snake will try to protect itself by biting you with its sharp, needlelike teeth.

What's this raccoon doing out during the day? It could have rabies, so stay away.

Some snakes are poisonous. They have fangs—long hollow teeth that inject venom when they bite. A poisonous snake uses its venom to kill prey and to protect itself from enemies. Some kinds of snakebites can make people very sick—or even kill them. If a snake ever bites you, tell an adult right away.

This poisonous rattlesnake is getting ready to strike.

A Plant that Stings!

Don't get too close to a nettle plant. Its prickly hairs will sting anything that brushes against them. Each stinging hair is hollow with a tiny, bulb-shaped tip that contains an irritating liquid. If you touch this plant, some of its hairs will break off and stick into your skin. Then the hairs will release their itchy fluid into your body.

You don't want to get too close to this nettle plant. If one of its stinging hairs touches you, your skin will itch terribly.

When you swim in the ocean, remember that you are not alone. There are millions of sea creatures trying to survive in their underwater world. If you get in their way, they may bite or sting you.

A shark's large, razor-sharp teeth can severely hurt or even kill a person. Movies such as *Jaws* have

The great white shark is one of the most dangerous sharks in the world. Fortunately, sharks are usually more interested in attacking other fish than people.

given sharks a bad reputation, but they rarely attack people. Sharks usually feed on smaller fish. Sometimes they bite a person in the midst of a feeding frenzy. When sharks are busy feeding on a large group of fish, they get so excited that they bite anything in sight. That's why you should never swim in a place where sharks are active.

Stingrays have a sharp spine on their tail. If you disturb a stingray, it will whip its tail against your legs or body. The spine on its tail will slice your skin and poison will flow into your body. The wound will probably swell up immediately. If you do not get medical attention right away, you may get very sick—or even die.

If you get in the way of a stingray, its whiplike tail may give you a painful sting.

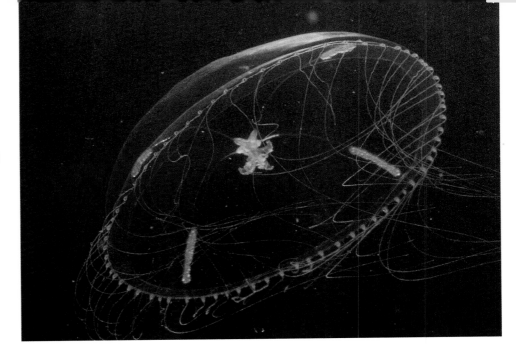

A jellyfish's tentacles look fine and delicate, but its sting is very painful.

The soft, fragile body of a jellyfish looks like an open umbrella. Its long, stinging **tentacles** hang down and paralyze fish and other prey that bump into them. The tentacles then drag the victim to the jellyfish's mouth. Some jellyfish are more dangerous than others. The sting of a Portuguese man-of-war is very painful. The tentacles of a jellyfish can sting even after they have broken off the animal's body! Be sure to watch out for them as you walk barefoot along the beach.

How Your Body Reacts

Most of the time, your skin does a good job of protecting you. It keeps harmful materials out of your body. When you get a bite or a sting, your skin is broken open and germs can sneak inside. Fortunately, your body has a special defense system that tells you when something is wrong and works hard to fix the damage.

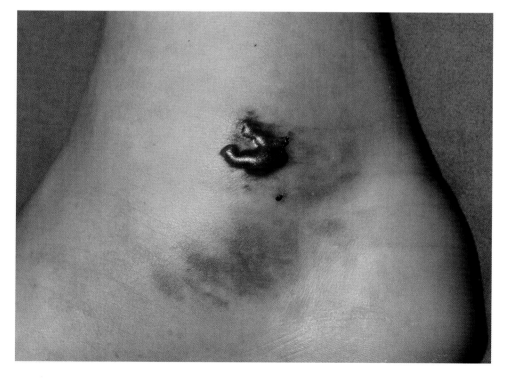

This snakebite has broken the skin and now germs can sneak in.

27

When your skin is wounded, chemicals pour out of the damaged cells. Some of these chemicals cause the walls of tiny blood vessels in your skin to leak. Fluid from your blood seeps out into the surrounding tissues, and your skin becomes red and swollen. This kind of body reaction is called **inflammation**.

The damaged cells also release chemicals that send out signals. These signals call in the body's defenders—the **white blood cells**. Most cells cannot move, but white blood cells can. They can squeeze out of tiny holes in the walls of blood vessels and swim through the fluid in the gaps between cells. The white blood cells act like a clean-up squad. When they come into contact with damaged tissue, they eat up dead cells and bits of dirt in the wound.

White blood cells also fight any **bacteria** that have entered the wound. They surround the bacteria and eat them. Some of the white blood cells die during the battle. Their dead bodies pile up to form **pus**.

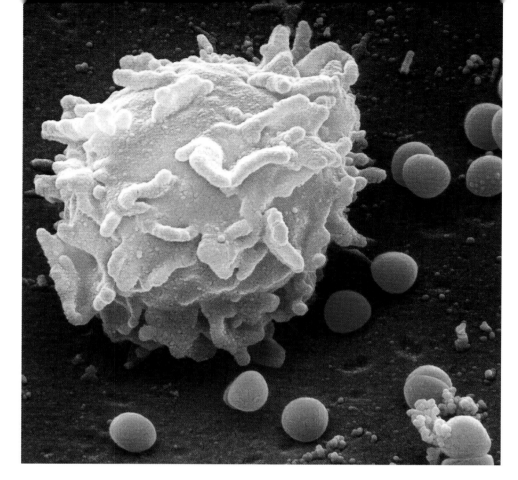

This white blood cell (blue) is getting ready to destroy bacteria.

The body keeps sending out more and more white blood cells until all the bacteria have been destroyed. As long as the battle goes on, your skin will stay red and swollen.

If the infection gets really bad, bacteria may spread to other parts of your body. This could make you very sick. If an infected bite or sting doesn't start to look better in 2 or 3 days, you should have it checked out by a doctor. You may need medicine to help bring the infection under control.

Activity 1: A Model of Infection

Dip a clean pin into a jar of peanut butter and drag it out *slowly* so that peanut butter sticks to the pin. Now stick the pin all the way into an orange and pull it out. Does any of the peanut butter get stuck inside the orange? Is any orange juice leaking out of the hole? When you squeeze the orange does any juice leak out?

When you stuck the pin into the orange, you made a wound like the kind you get from a bite or sting. Think of the orange as your body, the pin as a tooth or a stinger, and the peanut butter as bacteria. When you took the pin out, some of the peanut butter stayed inside the wound. The same thing happens when something thin and sharp punctures your skin. That's why **puncture wounds** often get infected.

When a Bite Makes You Sick

You probably know that bites can be painful, but did you know that some bites can make you very sick? Some animals carry disease germs that get into your body when they bite.

For example, mosquitoes can transmit **malaria** (muh-LAYR-ee-uh), a serious illness that is common in Africa, Asia, Central America, and South America.

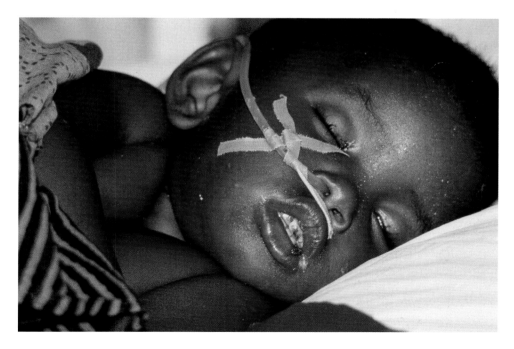

This child is suffering from malaria, which is transmitted through a mosquito bite.

A Surprising Sickness

In 1999, healthcare workers were surprised when a disease called West Nile fever suddenly appeared in New York City. This deadly disease usually occurs only in Africa. People soon realized that mosquitoes carrying West Nile fever had somehow been transported to the United States. Pesticides were sprayed over large areas of land to try to get rid of disease-carrying mosquitoes.

People with malaria often experience fever, chills, aches and pains, nausea, and sweating. If malaria is not treated, the person may die. If you travel to places where mosquitoes carry malaria, you need to take drugs that will help protect you from the disease.

A mosquito bite can also cause **encephalitis** (en-SEH-fuh-LYE-tuss), or inflammation of the brain. Encephalitis is a very serious illness. It can even lead to death. Most people with encephalitis experience painful headaches, a sore throat, a high fever, eye twitching, and slurred speech. Fortunately, this disease is rare in the United States. Only about 150 cases are reported each year.

Some ticks can also spread diseases. For example, the bacteria that cause **Lyme disease** are carried by deer ticks. This disease is spread when a tick injects its saliva—containing the bacterium—into its victim.

The first signs of Lyme disease often include flulike symptoms and a bull's-eye rash that forms around the tick bite. A person who gets Lyme disease and is not treated may develop more serious symptoms. Ticks can also carry other diseases, such as Rocky Mountain spotted fever, Texas cattle fever, encephalitis, and relapsing fever. Fortunately, most tick bites do not cause diseases.

Dog and cat bites can make you sick too. Dog bites sometimes become infected with **tetanus** bacteria. Deep puncture wounds allow these bacteria to thrive and multiply. Tetanus is sometimes called "lockjaw" because a person's jaw muscles may tighten up, making it hard to speak or eat. Other symptoms include fever, headache, sore throat, and stiff muscles. If tetanus is not treated right away, death is likely.

Did You Know...

The Lyme disease bacterium can make people, dogs, and cats very sick, but it does not harm deer ticks. It also has no effect on the two animals that deer ticks most often feed on—white-footed mice and deer.

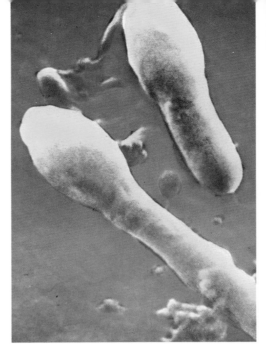

Animal bites can transmit germs that cause serious diseases. Here you see the bacteria that causes tetanus (left), and the viruses that cause rabies (right).

Dogs and cats can also spread rabies. The virus that causes rabies can be transmitted by an animal bite. It can also be spread if the animal's infected saliva gets into an open wound or the nose or eyes. Rabies destroys nerve cells in the brain.

In many states, the law requires that cats and dogs have shots to protect them against rabies. That means the pets are safe—and so are their owners. But you should always be careful around wild animals, especially raccoons, foxes, and bats. Many rabid animals become aggressive, snapping at everything or everyone. Some may act confused, stagger, or walk in circles. Others may seem healthy, but act unusually friendly toward people. It's hard to tell if an animal has rabies. So if any animal bites you, you should get medical help immediately. Rabies almost always kills if it is not treated quickly.

Cat-scratch disease is a mild illness caused by a bacterium in cat saliva. You can get the disease if an infected cat bites or scratches you. You may also get the illness by petting an infected cat and then rubbing your eye or touching your mouth. Symptoms include swollen lymph nodes, fever, tiredness, headache, and loss of appetite. Most people get better on their own in about 3 weeks, but a few develop serious problems such as encephalitis.

As you can see, bites can be very dangerous. If any animal bites you, tell an adult right away and get medical help.

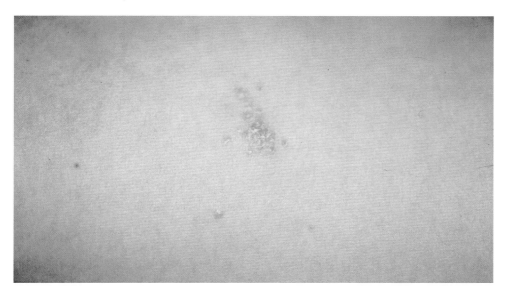

A scratch from a cat produced this rash.

Treating Bites and Stings

If you've been bitten by a poisonous spider or a snake—or stung by a scorpion or a stingray—you should see a doctor immediately. But many bites and stings can be treated at home.

Wash all insect bites thoroughly with soap and warm water. Ice or a cold compress may help to keep the swelling down. Try not to scratch insect bites. Scratching irritates the skin and may cause an infection.

The poisonous bite of a tiny recluse spider caused this serious wound.

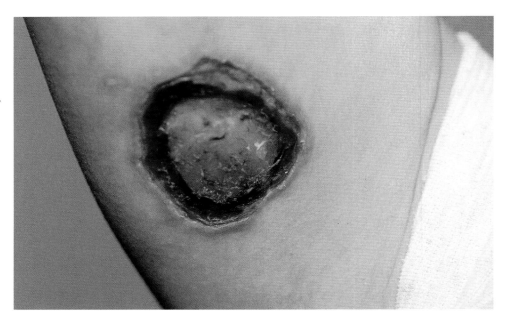

If a bee stings you, check to see whether the stinger is still in your skin. If it is, scrape it out with your fingernail. Don't use tweezers. They may squeeze out more venom and make the swelling worse. Products like After-Bite and Stingkill can help relieve the itching.

If the wound is very swollen, you may need to take an **antihistamine** (an-ti-HISS-tuh-MEEN)—a drug that helps reduce pain and swelling. You can also take Tylenol or other medicines that contain acetaminophen (uh-SEE-tuh-MIH-nuh-fun). If the swollen area around the wound feels numb, call a doctor.

People who are allergic to bee stings or spider bites may have breathing problems, faintness, clammy hands, or some other serious reaction. If this happens to you, go to the hospital immediately. You will be given a shot of **epinephrine** (eh-puh-NEH-frun)—a drug that can stop the allergic reaction and save your life.

This boy's eye is swollen shut after being stung by a yellow jacket.

How to Remove a Tick

If you find a tick attached to your skin, don't panic and rip it out with your fingers. Squeezing the tick may squirt more germs into your bite. Ask an adult to remove the tick.

Using tweezers, the adult should grasp the tick as close as possible to its mouthparts. It is important to avoid crushing the tick's swollen body. Once the tick has been removed, clean the bite thoroughly so that it will not get infected. To get rid of the tick, flush it down the toilet or put it inside a piece of sticky tape and throw it away.

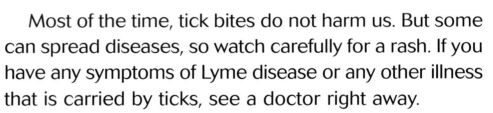

Most of the time, tick bites do not harm us. But some can spread diseases, so watch carefully for a rash. If you have any symptoms of Lyme disease or any other illness that is carried by ticks, see a doctor right away.

A deep animal bite can be very serious. It is extremely important to clean the wound with soap and water. Use an **antiseptic** (an-ti-SEP-tik) to kill any bacteria in the bite. Put some antibacterial ointment on the wound to help it heal. The wound should also be bandaged to protect it from further harm. If it has been more than 5 years since your last tetanus shot, it's probably a good idea to get a **booster** shot.

If the wound is bleeding, use a cloth to apply pressure to the area until the bleeding stops. If the wound is large, go to the hospital immediately. You may need stitches.

If you think you may have been bitten by an animal with rabies, call an animal control center. Tell them what bit you and how the animal behaved. They will try to find the animal and test it for rabies. In the meantime, you may have to get a series of rabies shots. Because rabies is a deadly disease, doctors believe that people should be treated right away.

A sting from an ocean creature can be very painful. Cold compresses can help the swelling. A doctor may need to give you a shot to ease the pain.

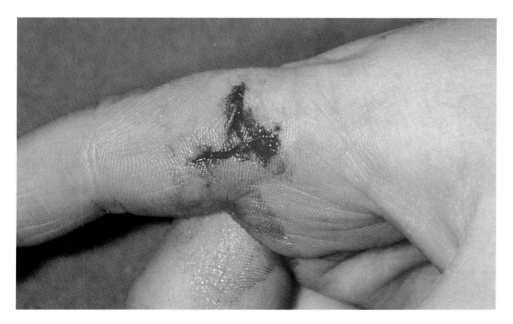

Animal bites need to be treated right away to avoid infection. You may also need shots to prevent rabies.

Activity 2: Make a Bite and Sting Survey

Just about everyone has been bitten by a mosquito, but how many people do you think have been stung by a bee? How common are dog and cat bites? To find out, you can do a survey. Ask your friends and neighbors the following questions:

1. Have you ever been bitten by an insect? What kinds of insects have bitten you? How many times have you been bitten by each kind of insect?

2. What kind of reactions did you have after the bites? Did your skin get red and swollen? How big was the sore? Did you feel faint or have trouble breathing? What did you do to treat the injury?

Ask the same kinds of questions about bites and stings from pets, wild animals, and ocean creatures. Which animals cause the most bites and stings? Which cause the most serious damage? If you have friends or relatives in other parts of North America, ask them the same questions and compare their answers with the results you got for your own area.

Protect Yourself!

As you can see, bites and stings can be dangerous. That's why you should try to protect yourself from creatures that may bite or sting you. If you follow a few simple rules, you will be less likely to be bitten and stung. These rules can spare you a lot of misery, and they might even save your life!

How to Avoid Insects and Ticks

- **Wear light-colored clothes and use insect repellent.**

- **Don't use sweet-smelling soaps or shampoos.**

- **Don't swat at wasps or bees, and stay away from their nests.**

- **Avoid playing in areas where there is standing water, such as ponds. Mosquitoes are most likely to be in such areas.**

- **When you walk in fields or in the woods, wear a long-sleeved shirt and long pants. Tuck your pants legs inside your socks. When you get home, ask an adult to check you for ticks.**

How to Avoid Animal Bites and Stings

- Don't tease a dog or make it angry.

- Never pet a strange dog or approach a wild animal— no matter how cute it looks.

- Don't swat at wasps or bees, and stay away from their nests.

- If you walk in wooded areas, watch out for snakes or any wild animals that are acting strangely.

- Never touch an injured animal.

- If you see an aggressive dog running around without a leash, call your local animal control center.

Glossary

abdomen—belly; the body part at the hind end of a spider, an insect, and some other animals

aggressive—hostile, likely to attack violently

allergic—having a tendency to overreact to a substance that is harmless to most people

antihistamine—a drug that blocks the action of histamine, a chemical that produces inflammation

antiseptic—a substance that prevents or slows down the growth of germs

bacterium (plural bacteria)—a germ; a single-celled organism too small to see without a microscope. Some bacteria cause diseases when they get into the body.

booster—an additional dose of a vaccine

bred—chose specific animals to mate in order to produce young with desirable characteristics

encephalitis—inflammation of the brain

epinephrine—a drug that helps to ease a severe allergic reaction

infect—to invade and damage body tissues

inflammation—redness, heat, and swelling that develop when tissues are damaged

Lyme disease—a disease caused by bacteria spread by tick bites

malaria—a disease caused by parasites spread by mosquitoes

prey—an animal hunted and killed for food by another animal

proboscis—the needlelike beak of an insect

puncture wound—a small but deep hole cut into the skin by a sharp, pointed object

pus—a thick, white or yellow substance that is made up of dead white blood cells and bacteria

rabies—a deadly disease caused by a virus that is transmitted from an infected animal

saliva—the watery fluid that forms in the mouth and helps in chewing and swallowing food

tentacle—a long, stringy stinging structure found in jellyfish and some other animals

tetanus—a dangerous disease caused by bacteria that grow inside a puncture wound

venom—poison produced by an animal such as a spider, a bee, a wasp, or a snake

white blood cell—a blood cell that can move through tissues; an important part of the body's defense system

wound—an injury

Learning More

Books

Artell, Mike. *Backyard Bloodsuckers: Questions, Facts, and Tongue Twisters About Creepy, Crawly Creatures*. Parsippany, NJ: Good Year Books, 2000.

Fredericks, Anthony D. *Animal Sharpshooters*. Danbury, CT: Franklin Watts, 1999.

Souza, D. M. *What Bit Me?* Minneapolis, MN: Carolrhoda Books, Inc., 1991.

Stewart, Melissa. *Insects*. Danbury, CT: Children's Press, 2001.

Organizations and Online Sites

American Academy of Allergy, Asthma and Immunology
611 East Wells Street
Milwaukee, Wisconsin 53202

Bites and Scratches
http://kidshealth.org/parent/firstaid/bites.html
This site explains how to treat bites and scratches.

Bites and Stings
http://www.mayohealth.org/mayo/firstaid/htm/fasub2.htm
This site is maintained by the Mayo Foundation. It features lots of links to information about bites and stings and how to treat them.

Common First-Aid Procedures: Bites and Stings
http://cpmcnet.columbia.edu/texts/guide/hmg14_0004.html
This Web page is part of the Columbia University Web site. It has up-to-date information about bites and stings and describes popular treatments.

Ouch! Itch! What to Do When You're Bugged by Bugs
http://kidshealth.org/kid/ill_injure/aches/bug_bites.html
This site features easy-to-understand information about insects. It also explains how to treat an insect bite or sting.

Summertime Update on Bites and Stings
http://www.convoke.com:80/markjr/summer.html
This site describes some of the most serious symptoms that can result from bites and stings and explains how to treat them.

U.S. Fish and Wildlife Service
1849 C. Street, N.W.
Washington, DC 20240

U.S. Public Health Service
Centers for Disease Control
   and Prevention
1600 Clifton Road
Atlanta, GA 30333

Index

About the Authors

Dr. Alvin Silverstein is a professor of biology at the College of Staten Island of the City University of New York. Virginia B. Silverstein is a translator of Russian scientific literature. The Silversteins first worked together on a research project at the University of Pennsylvania. Since then, they have produced 6 children and more than 160 published books for young people.

Laura Silverstein Nunn, a graduate of Kean College, has been helping with her parents' books since her high-school days. She is the coauthor of more than thirty books on diseases and health, science concepts, endangered species, and pets. Laura lives with her husband Matt and their young son Cory in a rural New Jersey town not far from her childhood home.